W9-BCN-841

Kevin Garnett

Champion Basketball Star

Stew Thornley

E **Enslow Publishers, Inc.**
40 Industrial Road
Box 398
Berkeley Heights, NJ 07922
USA

http://www.enslow.com

Original edition published as *Super Sports Star Kevin Garnett* in 2001.

Library of Congress Cataloging-in-Publication Data

Thornley, Stew.
  Kevin Garnett : champion basketball star / Stew Thornley.
    p. cm. — (Sports star champions)
  Includes index.
  Summary: "Explores basketball player Kevin Garnett, including his childhood, NBA career for the Minnesota Timberwolves, winning a championship with the Boston Celtics, and how he became an all-time great in the NBA"— Provided by publisher.
  ISBN 978-0-7660-4028-1
  1. Garnett, Kevin, 1976– —Juvenile literature. 2. Basketball players—United States—Biography—Juvenile literature. I. Title.
  GV884.G3T47 2013
  796.323092—dc23
  [B]
                              2011031517
Future editions:
Paperback ISBN 978-1-4644-0157-2
ePUB ISBN 978-1-4645-1064-9
PDF ISBN 978-1-4646-1064-6

032012 Lake Book Manufacturing, Inc., Melrose Park, IL

Printed in the United States of America

10 9 8 7 6 5 4 3 2 1

To Our Readers: We have done our best to make sure all Internet addresses in this book were active and appropriate when we went to press. However, the author and the publisher have no control over and assume no liability for the material available on those Internet sites or on other Web sites they may link to. Any comments or suggestions can be sent by e-mail to comments@enslow.com or to the address on the back cover.

♻ Enslow Publishers, Inc., is committed to printing our books on recycled paper. The paper in every book contains 10% to 30% post-consumer waste (PCW). The cover board on the outside of each book contains 100% PCW. Our goal is to do our part to help young people and the environment too!

Illustration Credits: AP Images, p. 26; AP Images / Andy King, pp. 35, 36; AP Images / Charles Bennett, p. 23; AP Images / Charles Krupa, pp. 8, 12, 19, 20, 41; AP Images / Elise Amendola, p. 38; AP Images / Frank Franklin II, p. 42; AP Images / Kathy Willens, p. 1; AP Images / Kevork Djansezian, p. 6; AP Images / Mark Duncan, p. 14; AP Images / Mark J. Terrill, p. 34; AP Images / Rich Pedroncelli, p. 32; AP Images / Scott Troyanos, p. 28; AP Images / Tom Strattman, p. 30; AP Images / Winslow Townson, pp. 4, 5, 9, 17.

Cover Illustration: AP Images / Kathy Willens (Kevin Garnett).

Contents

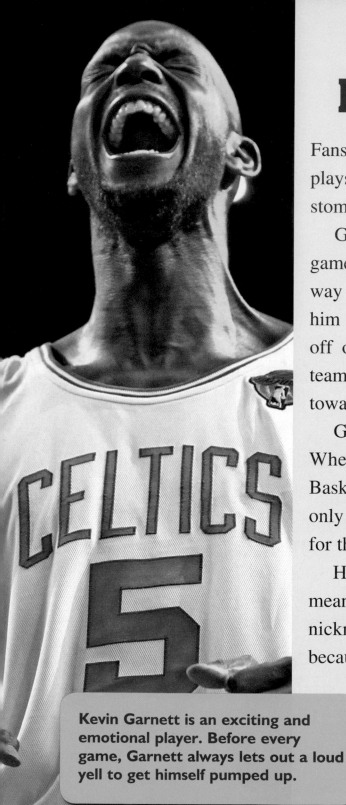

Kevin Garnett is an exciting and emotional player. Before every game, Garnett always lets out a loud yell to get himself pumped up.

Introduction

Fans get excited when Kevin Garnett plays. They cheer, scream, clap, and stomp their feet.

Garnett also gets excited during games. When he dunks, he yells on his way down from the basket. It keeps him pumped up. This excitement rubs off on his teammates. As one of his teammates said, "Kevin's enthusiasm toward the game is something special."

Garnett plays for the Boston Celtics. When he started in the National Basketball Association (NBA), he was only nineteen years old. He then played for the Minnesota Timberwolves.

He was known as "Da Kid," which means "the kid." Soon, he had another nickname, the "Big Ticket." That's because a ticket to see Da Kid play was worth a lot. Garnett is called many things, including his initials. Sometimes he even yells them at himself. "C'mon, KG," he hollers when he misses a shot.

Another thing KG is called is a winner. He helped the Timberwolves to become a winning team. Later, he went to Boston and helped them improve and win a championship.

Garnett plays a position called power forward. A power forward has to be able to grab rebounds for his team. He has to be able to block shots and play good defense. Garnett does all these things well.

He can also do the things expected of other positions. He scores a lot of points. He passes to teammates so they can score. He even handles the ball well. Power forwards of the past didn't have so many different skills. Today, more players can do more things. Garnett led the way for a new type of power forward.

For many years, Kevin Garnett has been one of the best players in the NBA.

Kevin Garnett plays power forward for the Boston Celtics.

Kevin Garnett (right) blocks a shot during Game 3 of the 2008 NBA Finals. Garnett's outstanding play helped lead the Celtics to the NBA championship.

A Champion at Last

Kevin Garnett is used to hearing cheers from the fans. Sometimes it is when he makes a basket, grabs a rebound, or blocks a shot. Sometimes it is when he comes into a game. On June 17, 2008, he heard the cheers when he came out of a game.

The Boston Celtics had a 116–81 lead over the Los Angeles Lakers. Just over four minutes remained in Game 6 of the NBA Finals. When it was over, the Celtics would be champions. Boston coach Glenn "Doc" Rivers took Garnett out, along with two other stars, Paul Pierce and Ray Allen. It was not just that they were not needed anymore. It was so the fans could stand and cheer as they came off the court.

Kevin Garnett attempts a shot over Los Angeles Lakers forward Lamar Odom during Game 6 of the 2008 NBA Finals. Garnett had 26 points and 14 rebounds in the victory that clinched the Celtics their seventeenth NBA championship.

These three All-Star players were leading the Celtics to their first championship in more than twenty years. It was a special moment for all of them. For the man they call "KG," it was more than that.

Kevin Garnett (left center) holds the Larry O'Brien Trophy after winning the 2008 NBA championship. He is celebrating with his teammates Ray Allen (right), Paul Pierce (center), and Glen "Big Baby" Davis (left).

Garnett had come into the NBA more than ten years ago. The team that drafted him, the Minnesota Timberwolves, was not a good team. But Garnett helped them improve. The team never won a championship, though. And that's something Garnett wanted more than anything else.

He played great in this game. However, it was not about him. It was about the team. Garnett had received honors for himself before. Now he shared his joy with his teammates.

Garnett, Pierce, and Allen hugged one another as they came out of the game. A few minutes later, everyone was hugging. The Celtics won the game, 131–92. The Boston fans chanted, "We Beat L.A.!"

Garnett was feeling it all. He went to center court and kissed the drawing of the leprechaun that is part of the Celtics' symbol. "Other than my kid being born," he said, "this has got to be the happiest day of my life right now."

Spending Time on the Court

Kevin Garnett was born on May 19, 1976. He grew up in Mauldin, South Carolina, a small town near Greenville.

Kevin's dad, O'Lewis McCullough, had been a good basketball player. McCullough had been known as "Bye-Bye 45." His number in high school was 45, and he was very fast. He would steal the ball and take off running down the court toward the basket. When that happened, it was "Bye-Bye 45."

Kevin's father did not live with him, though. Ernest Irby was Kevin's stepfather. Irby did not like basketball. He would not let Kevin have a basketball hoop in the driveway.

As a kid, Kevin played basketball against his friend Baron "Bear" Franks. Because Bear was older, it was a difficult challenge for Kevin. But this made him a tougher player. Garnett is known as one of the toughest defenders in the NBA.

That did not keep Kevin from playing basketball, though. He loved the game.

Baron Franks was one of Kevin Garnett's friends. Franks said about Garnett, "All he did was talk about basketball. And every time you saw him, he had a ball. Sun up. Sun down. Up and down the street. All day long."

Franks was known as "Bear." He was several years older than Garnett. He was also bigger. Kevin and Bear would often play basketball against each other. Bear would not go easy on Kevin. He wore Kevin out on the court. Kevin sometimes wondered if Franks liked him. Franks did like Kevin, but he wanted to help him improve his game. The tough treatment on the court was his way of teaching Kevin. And Kevin did get better. He also got tougher. Playing against Bear helped him a lot.

Kevin also played basketball with other friends at Springfield Park in Mauldin. Kevin's best friend was Jaime Peters, who was known as "Bug." Kevin and Bug were about the same age. Their houses were across the street from one another in Mauldin.

Bug was small and not very good at basketball. But he knew that Kevin had talent. He encouraged Kevin to play basketball. The two went to Springfield Park all the time.

Kevin Garnett shoots during practice before an NBA Finals game. When he was growing up in Mauldin, Kevin spent a lot of time at the park shooting baskets. He practiced even after the sun went down, under the lights.

Kevin would practice for hours at the park. Even after everyone else left, Kevin stayed. He would shoot baskets by himself under the lights.

Kevin also had other things to do besides play basketball. He took care of his younger sister, Ashley. Kevin also had an older sister, Sonya. Their mother, Shirley, worked two jobs to support them. She worked in a factory and also had a hair-styling business. She was away from home a lot, so Kevin helped out with his younger sister.

Kevin still found lots of time to play basketball, though. He could not get enough of it. When he was in ninth grade, his first year of high school, he tried out for the high school team. His mother did not even know he had tried out. By the time she found out, Kevin had already made the team.

Playing to Win

Kevin Garnett was tall when he started high school. In ninth grade, he was six feet seven inches tall. He was already a good defensive player. With his long arms, he could easily block shots. He could also jump and grab rebounds, too.

He needed to work on his offense, though. He worked hard to improve, and it paid off. His coach at Mauldin High School was James "Duke" Fisher. Coach Fisher taught Garnett how to dribble, pass, and shoot. The coach was impressed with how hard Garnett worked to improve. Garnett had a good year during his first high school season. He scored an average of 12.5 points per game. Garnett also

Kevin Garnett makes a pass during a game against the Detroit Pistons. When Kevin got to high school, he was already a great defender and rebounder. However, his offensive game needed extra practice.

averaged 14 rebounds and 7 blocked shots. Those were good totals, but Kevin was only getting started.

Coach Fisher said Kevin was a team player. "He didn't care who scored," said Fisher. "That is the truth. The only thing he hated was to lose." With Kevin playing, the Mauldin Mavericks did not lose much.

Fans in Mauldin were excited about the team. By Kevin's third year in high school, it was hard to get a ticket to see the team play. The gym at Mauldin High School was full for every game. Many fans could not get into the gym. They crowded into the hallway outside the gym. They could not see the game, but they could hear it. That was good enough for them.

In his third year in high school, Kevin averaged 27 points, 17 rebounds, and 7 blocks. He was named Mr. Basketball for South Carolina. Mr. Basketball is the award given to the best high school player in the state.

Kevin played basketball all year. He even played in a summer league. His coach in that league was Darren "Bull" Gazaway. Coach Gazaway had been coaching summer basketball for many years. He put together a great team in 1994, the summer after Kevin's third year in high school.

The team went to the Kentucky Hoopfest Tournament held in Louisville. Other great teams from many states came, too. But the team that Kevin played on was the best. Kevin's team won the Hoopfest championship.

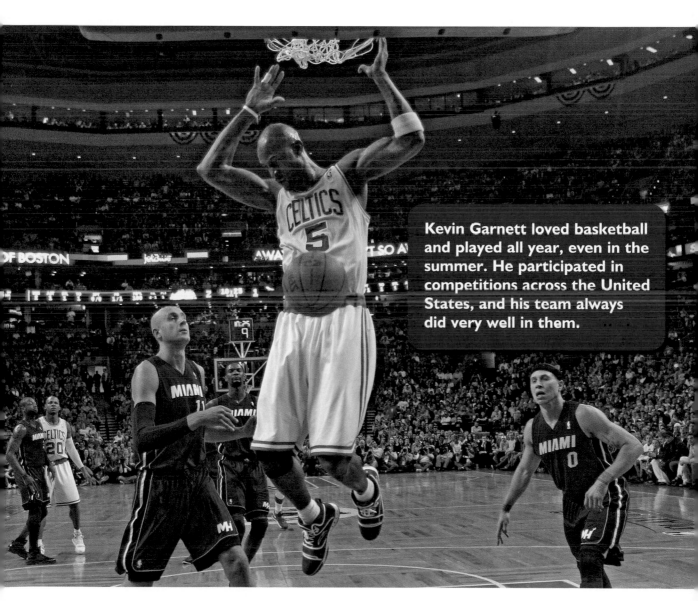

Kevin Garnett loved basketball and played all year, even in the summer. He participated in competitions across the United States, and his team always did very well in them.

Kevin Garnett salutes the crowd during the fourth quarter of a game against the Charlotte Bobcats. Garnett became accustomed to playing in front of large crowds in high school because his games in both Mauldin and Chicago often sold out.

Kevin also played in many other competitions around the United States. The teams were put together with the best high school players in the country. Kevin did well in these tournaments. He attracted a lot of attention.

But Kevin was a private person. He did not like all the attention. He wanted to blend in. He found a way to do that when he changed to a high school in a much larger city. Kevin, his mother, and younger sister moved to Chicago. He attended Farragut Academy.

Farragut's coach was William "Wolf" Nelson. Kevin Garnett had met him in the summer of 1994, at a basketball camp in Chicago. Kevin decided he would like to play for Coach Nelson.

Kevin Garnett and his family even lived in the same apartment building where Coach Nelson lived. It was not in a nice part of town, though. There were street gangs in the area. It was not safe to go out alone at night. Kevin learned it was different from Mauldin, South Carolina, where he could go to the park at night. In Chicago, he had to stay home.

Chicago is the home of the Bears football team. The Bears are known as "Da Bears." It is also home to the Chicago Bulls basketball team. The Bulls are known as "Da Bulls."

When Kevin got to Chicago, he became known as "Da Kid." It is a nickname he still has today.

One of Kevin's teammates at Farragut was Ronnie Fields. Kevin had met Fields at a basketball camp in Chicago. Ronnie Fields was a great jumper, and he also had some interesting moves.

With Kevin and Ronnie Fields, the Farragut Admirals team was one of the best in the state. It was even one of the top teams in the country.

Kevin was again the leader of his team. He was still playing in front of large crowds. In January 1995, Farragut played against a good team from the town of Rock Island, near Chicago. More than five thousand fans were at the Farragut gym for the game. Ronnie and Kevin put on a great show. Ronnie had some amazing dunks. But Kevin also thrilled the fans with a few slam dunks. He scored 23 points and had 19 rebounds in the game. Farragut beat Rock Island by twelve points.

Kevin again played well a few weeks later. The Admirals were playing Carver High School of Chicago in a championship game. Kevin had 32 points and 13 rebounds. Farragut won, 71–62.

Kevin Garnett answers questions from reporters after announcing his decision to go pro straight out of high school on May 15, 1995. He was only the fourth player in history to go from high school directly to the NBA.

The Farragut Admirals went to the state tournament. The team did not win, but Kevin played well. When the season was over, Kevin was named Mr. Basketball for Illinois. He had now won that award in South Carolina and Illinois.

Everyone knew Kevin Garnett was a great star. Now he had to make a choice. Would he go to college or begin to play professional basketball?

Teams from the NBA had been watching him. A lot of teams wanted Kevin to play for them. He decided he would play basketball in the NBA. "I went with my heart," he said.

Many people did not think Garnett was ready to play with the pros. Some people thought he was making a mistake by not going to college first. But Garnett knew he could prove them wrong.

A Hot Rookie

The NBA draft is the way that professional basketball teams choose new players each year. Teams take turns picking players. During the June 1995 draft, there were a lot of good players waiting to be chosen. Damon Stoudamire, Joe Smith, Antonio McDyess, and Jerry Stackhouse were among them. They had all played basketball in college. Kevin Garnett was different. He was coming to the NBA right after high school.

Even so, Garnett was the fifth player selected in the draft. The Minnesota Timberwolves picked him. They thought he would become a great player, maybe even a superstar. But they knew that would not happen right away.

The Minnesota Timberwolves selected Kevin Garnett as the fifth player in the first round of the 1995 NBA Draft. In this photo, Garnett shakes hands with NBA Commissioner David Stern on draft day.

The Timberwolves wanted Garnett to get used to playing in the NBA. He would be playing against better players than the ones he had seen in high school. He would also travel a lot. And he would be living in Minnesota, far away from his family. All this would be new to Garnett.

Garnett spent a lot of time sitting on the sideline, not playing. However, when he got the chance, he showed how good he could be. A few weeks into the 1995 season, Minnesota played the Vancouver Grizzlies. Early in the second quarter, a Vancouver player missed a shot. Garnett grabbed the rebound. He turned and threw a pass out of the crowd of players. Then he raced down the court. His long legs carried him past defenders. Garnett crossed midcourt. He looked for the ball. A teammate threw a pass to him. Garnett caught it, got set, and took a shot. The long, three-point shot dropped through the basket.

Garnett's great play excited the other players on the Timberwolves. Minnesota went on to win the game by more than twenty points.

Garnett was showing a lot of people that he could play in the NBA. A game between Houston and Minnesota in March 1996 proved Garnett was ready for the NBA. The score was close in the fourth quarter, then Garnett got going.

Kevin Garnett blocks a shot during a game against the Phoenix Suns in his rookie season. As a rookie in the NBA, Garnett had a lot to learn. But it did not take long for him to show how good he could be.

He scored nine straight points in two minutes. In that time, he also had two rebounds and two blocked shots.

During the 1995–1996 season, the Timberwolves traded Christian Laettner to the Atlanta Hawks. The trade opened up a spot in the starting lineup. Timberwolves' coach Phil "Flip" Saunders thought Garnett was the man to fill that spot. So Garnett got more playing time. Three weeks later, Garnett scored 33 points in a game against the Boston Celtics.

Garnett started in all of Minnesota's games over the last half of the season. During that time, he averaged 14 points per game.

"The first time I saw him work out, I thought he had a chance to be great," said Coach Saunders. But Garnett was becoming a great player even faster than Saunders thought he would.

After the Minnesota Timberwolves traded away Christian Laettner, Garnett was thrust into the starting lineup. He was a dominant force on the offensive and defensive ends of the floor.

Making It in Minnesota

Kevin Garnett went from "Da Kid" to a man in a hurry. He became the leader of the Minnesota Timberwolves. He also showed everyone in basketball how good he was.

In 1999–2000, Kevin averaged 22.9 points per game. He also averaged 11.8 rebounds and 5 assists. This made him a 20-10-5 player. That means he had those average totals in these important categories. He was consistent. He is the only player in NBA history to average those numbers for six straight seasons.

He also stood out in other ways. Garnett was voted to the starting lineup for the West squad in the 2003 All-Star Game. Michael Jordan, one of the NBA's all-time greats,

Kevin Garnett quickly became Minnesota's most important player and one of the best forwards in the league. His fadeaway jump shot became an unstoppable move.

was playing in his final All-Star Game. Jordan got a lot of the attention, but Garnett grabbed the spotlight.

The East led by ten points in the final minutes, but KG helped the West battle back. The game went into overtime. Jordan put the East ahead with 4.8 seconds left, but the West ticd it. For the first time, an All-Star Game was going to double overtime.

Garnett made sure it would go no further than that. He scored the first seven points in the second overtime. The West won, 155–145. He finished with 37 points, 9 rebounds, and 5 steals. As one legend, Michael Jordan, was going out, another was stepping up to take his place.

The Timberwolves were making the playoffs during these years. However, they kept losing in the opening round. Garnett wanted his team to go deeper. He wanted to win a NBA title.

KG was as good as anyone could be in 2003–2004. He averaged more than 24 points per game during the regular season. He also led the league in rebounding. It was the first of four seasons in a row that he accomplished that feat. Few players had done that before. Garnett was named the NBA's Most Valuable Player for the season.

Kevin Garnett has been selected to the All-Star team fourteen times. He won the All-Star Game MVP award in 2003. In this photo, Garnett jumps to block a shot against Shaquille O'Neal during the 2007 All-Star Game.

"He amazes me every year because he always comes back better," said his coach, Flip Saunders.

But Garnett played even better in the playoffs. For the first time, the Timberwolves won a playoff series, beating the Denver Nuggets. Next, they faced the Sacramento Kings. The winner of this series would advance to the Western Conference Finals.

The Timberwolves and the Kings battled fiercely, and the series came down to an all-important seventh game. In the big game, the best player dominated. KG scored 32 points and had 21 rebounds. He also blocked 5 shots and had 4 steals. The Timberwolves won, 83–80.

KG waves a towel on top of the scorer's table celebrating with fans after defeating the Sacramento Kings in the 2004 Western Conference Semifinals.

In 2003–2004, Garnett had an incredible individual season and was named the NBA Most Valuable Player. Garnett holds the MVP award while speaking to the Minnesota Timberwolves' fans on May 4, 2004, after receiving the trophy.

"There was a ton of pressure," said Saunders, "but he had an amazing calm about him."

The Timberwolves next faced the Los Angeles Lakers. The Lakers were too much for the Wolves and won the series. It had been a great year for Garnett and his team, but he wanted more. He still wanted that title.

Over the next several years, Garnett was at the top of his game. However, the rest of the team wasn't keeping up. The Timberwolves didn't make the playoffs again.

Minnesota decided it was time to rebuild its team with other players. Meanwhile, a different team in the NBA was looking to add another superstar.

Kevin Garnett (center) jokes with teammates Ray Allen (left) and Paul Pierce on the Boston Celtics' bench. After Garnett was traded to Boston, critics and fans wondered if he and fellow All-Stars Pierce and Allen could play together. But the Big Three, as they are called, immediately bonded and the Celtics became a great team.

CHAPTER SIX

Winning It All

Don Nelson, a former coach in the NBA, once said of KG, "Garnett makes plays for everybody else and dominates that way."

The Boston Celtics had a team that needed some help. A team with a rich history, the Celtics had won sixteen NBA championships. But in 2006–2007, the Celtics were awful. They had one All-Star player, Paul Pierce, but they needed to add more. Boston needed a player who was not only good himself, but one who could also make his teammates better.

In the summer of 2007, the Celtics acquired Ray Allen, an outstanding shooting guard. A month later, the Celtics made a big trade with the Timberwolves. Boston gave up five players and two future picks in the draft to get one player. At that time, it was the most players ever traded for a single player. That player was Kevin Garnett.

Some people thought the Celtics now had too many stars. Pierce, Allen, and Garnett had always been the best players on their teams. Could they share the ball? Could they work together?

The three already knew each other. They had played in a high school tournament in the early 1990s that had the best players from around the country competing against each other. As teammates on the Celtics, each was determined to win for the team, not for himself.

Boston improved a lot in 2007–2008. The Celtics won sixty-six games during the regular season. That was forty-two more than the year before. Garnett's personal numbers went down. That's because he was on a team that had other great players.

The Celtics had a stifling defense that season. They held their opponents to the worst shooting percentage in the league. On defense, Garnett was the best of the bunch. He was named the Defensive Player of the Year in the NBA.

The Celtics made the playoffs. They beat three teams to reach the NBA Finals. They hadn't won a title since 1986.

KG steals the ball from Sebastian Telfair during a game against Garnett's former team, the Minnesota Timberwolves. Garnett's arrival in Boston transformed their team into a defensive powerhouse, and Garnett won the Defensive Player of the Year award in 2008.

Although Kevin Garnett has secured his place as one of the NBA's all-time greats, he continues to work hard and wants to win another NBA championship.

Up Close!

During the summer, Garnett runs along the beach. He sets a water bottle in the sand and then runs a long distance down the beach. Only when he runs back does he get to pick up the bottle and take a drink. Asked if he likes running on the beach, Garnett said, "Nah, but I do love getting better."

Winning this year wouldn't be easy. They played the Los Angeles Lakers. The Celtics and Lakers have had a great rivalry for fifty years. Lately, the Lakers had been winning more. That didn't bother Garnett. He was ready.

Playing in Boston, the Celtics won the first two games. They went to Los Angeles for the next three games and won only one of those.

The series came back to Boston. If the Lakers won the next game, there would be a seventh game. But that didn't happen. Garnett and Ray Allen each scored 26 points. KG also had 14 rebounds. The Lakers didn't have a chance. Boston won the game, 131–92. Garnett had reached his goal of winning a title. The Celtics were champions. Since then, Garnett plays, and works, as hard as ever. The Celtics made it back to the NBA Finals in 2010. They played the Lakers again. This time the Lakers won.

New stars and strong teams are in the NBA. The Miami Heat are like the Celtics in that they have three All-Star players: LeBron James, Dwyane Wade, and Chris Bosh. In 2011, Miami beat the Celtics in the playoffs.

The Celtics and Garnett are still going strong, though. And Garnett is doing what the Celtics wanted. He plays great ball, and he helps others.

"You see the intensity out there on the court, but he's a wonderful man," teammate Glen Davis said of KG. "He's helped me tremendously."

He works hard as a player, but Garnett is a family man, too. He and his wife, Brandi, have a daughter who was born in 2008. He spends as much time as he can with them.

He still works hard to stay in shape. Garnett has achieved a lot already, but he still wants to win another championship.

Career Statistics

NBA Regular-Season Statistics with Minnesota Timberwolves from 1995–1996 to 2006–2007
NBA Regular-Season Statistics with Boston Celtics from 2007–2008 to 2010–2011

Year	GP	Min.	FGM	FGA	FG%	FT%	Reb.	Ast.	Stl.	Blk.	Pts.	PPG
1995–1996	80	2,293	361	735	.491	.705	501	145	86	131	835	10.4
1996–1997	77	2,995	549	1,100	.499	.754	618	236	105	163	1,309	17.0
1997–1998	82	3,222	635	1,293	.491	.738	786	348	139	150	1,518	18.5
1998–1999	47	1,780	414	900	.460	.704	489	202	78	83	977	20.8
1999–2000	81	3,243	759	1,526	.497	.765	956	401	120	126	1,857	22.9
2000–2001	81	3,202	704	1,475	.477	.764	921	401	111	145	1,784	22.0
2001–2002	81	3,175	659	1,401	.470	.801	981	422	96	126	1,714	21.2
2002–2003	82	3,321	743	1,481	.502	.751	1102	495	113	129	1,883	23.0
2003–2004	82	3,231	804	1,611	.499	.791	1139	409	120	178	1,987	24.2
2004–2005	82	3,121	683	1,360	.502	.811	1108	466	121	112	1,817	22.2
2005–2006	76	2,957	626	1,191	.526	.810	966	308	104	107	1,656	21.8
2006–2007	76	2,995	638	1,341	.476	.835	975	313	89	126	1,704	22.4
2007–2008	71	2,328	534	990	.539	.801	655	244	100	89	1,337	18.8
2008–2009	57	1,772	393	740	.531	.841	485	144	63	68	899	15.8
2009–2010	69	2,060	402	772	.521	.837	506	185	68	57	990	14.3
2010–2011	71	2,220	434	822	.528	.862	631	171	95	57	1,056	14.9
Totals	1,195	43,915	9,338	18,738	.498	.788	12,819	4,890	1,608	1,847	23,323	19.5

GP–Games Played
Min.–Minutes Played
FGM–Field Goals Made

FGA–Field Goals Attempted
FG%–Field Goal Percentage
FT%–Free Throw Percentage

Reb.–Rebounds
Ast.–Assists
Stl.–Steals

Blk.–Blocked Shots
Pts.–Points Scored
PPG–Points per Game

Where to Write to Kevin Garnett

Mr. Kevin Garnett
c/o Boston Celtics
226 Causeway Street, Fourth Floor
Boston, Massachusetts 02114

Glossary

assist—A pass to a teammate who makes a basket.

draft—The way NBA teams choose new players each year.

dunk—A shot that is slammed through the basket from directly above the basket. It is also known as a slam or slam dunk.

fadeaway—A shot taken while falling away from the basket.

rebound—Grabbing the basketball after a missed shot.

rookie—First-year player in a league.

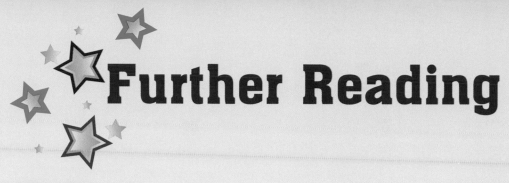# Further Reading

Books

Edwards, Ethan. *Meet Kevin Garnett: Basketball's Big Ticket.* New York: PowerKids Press, 2009.

Fedorko, Jamie. *Kevin Garnett.* Philadelphia: Mason Crest Publishers, 2009.

Ladewski, Paul. *Stars on the Court.* New York: Scholastic Inc., 2009.

Woods, Mark. *Basketball Legends.* New York: Crabtree Publishing Company, 2009.

Zuehlke, Jeffrey. *Kevin Garnett.* Minneapolis, Minn.: Lerner Publications, 2010.

Internet Addresses

ESPN.com: Kevin Garnett Player Profile
<http://espn.go.com/nba/player/_/id/261/kevin-garnett>

NBA.com
<http://www.nba.com/home/index.html>

The Official Web site of the Boston Celtics
<http://www.nba.com/celtics/>

Index